Christmas Baking

Fun and Delicious

Holiday Treats

Text and Recipes: MIA ÖHRN
Photos: ULRIKA POUSETTE

Translated by MONIKA ROMARE

Skyhorse Publishing

Originally published by ICA bokförlag, Forma Books AB
Translated by Monika Romare

Skyhorse Publishing books may be purchased in bulk at special discounts for sales
promotion, corporate gifts, fund-raising, or educational purposes. Special editions can
also be created to specifications. For details, contact the Special Sales Department,
Skyhorse Publishing, 307 West 36th Street, 11th Floor, New York, NY 10018
or info@skyhorsepublishing.com.

Skyhorse® and Skyhorse Publishing® are registered trademarks of
Skyhorse Publishing, Inc.®, a Delaware corporation.

www.skyhorsepublishing.com

10 9 8 7 6 5 4 3 2 1

Library of Congress Cataloging-in-Publication
Data is available on file.

ISBN: 978-1-61608-822-4

Printed in China

Merry Christmas!

There is probably nothing nicer than having your kitchen filled with the aroma of freshly-baked treats during Advent. When it's dark and chilly outside, there is nothing better than cozying up inside by the fireplace and smelling the spicy scents of gingerbread, mulled wine, and saffron. This time of year, many people that usually don't bake at home take the opportunity to do so. Therefore, I think it's especially important to have simple recipes that are easy to follow on hand. If you get stressed about all the other things that need to be prepared before Christmas Eve, just like I always do, I recommend the gingerbread chocolate. It's super tasty and can be made in the blink of an eye. If you would rather take on a bit of a challenge, the chocolate pastries with the blood orange cream or the gingerbread house are good choices. Whatever recipe you choose, it's one of my favorites, carefully selected to give you an extra merry Christmas.

Table of Contents

Candy

Toffee Lollipops

Create some variety by pouring half of the batter into toffee molds and the other half into small paper cones. Stick cocktail sticks into them, and you'll have beautiful toffee lollipops. You can see the toffee on page 36.

❊ 8–10 lollipops and about 25 small toffees

⅓ cup (50 g) flaked or chopped almonds
⅘ cup (200 ml) whipping cream
⅘ cup (280 g) light corn syrup
⅘ cup (180 g) granulated sugar

1. Lightly crumble the almonds.

2. Bring the whipping cream, syrup, and sugar to a boil in a wide saucepan with a thick bottom. Lower to medium heat once the mixture has boiled, and simmer on medium heat until the toffee has reached 252°F (122°C) and passes the cold water caramel test (see below). Stir the mixture occasionally. Meanwhile, place toffee molds on a tray.

3. Remove the pan from heat and stir the almonds into the batter.

4. Spoon the toffee into the molds and allow to cool. If you want to make lollipops: fold small pieces of greaseproof paper into cones, staple them, place them in small glasses, and fill with the toffee batter. Press little cocktail sticks into the cones. Store in the refrigerator.

COLD WATER CARAMEL TEST

Do a cold water caramel test by dropping a little bit of the batter into a glass of ice-cold water. Wait a few seconds and then try to shape the dough into a ball. This allows you to check the consistency of the toffee once it has cooled. If the ball is too soft, you will need to boil the toffee a little bit longer.

Lingonberry Toffee

*Sweet, tangy, and perfectly chewy. You can vary this toffee by replacing
the lingonberries with cranberries, strawberries, blueberries, currants, or any other berries you like.*

about 30 toffees

⅖ cup (100 g) frozen and thawed lingonberries, or other berries
(or fresh when in season)
⅗ cup (150 ml) whipping cream
1 cup (225 g) granulated sugar
1 tbsp light corn syrup

neutral cooking oil for the baking dish

1. Place parchment paper on a 6 x 6 inch (15 x 15 cm) pan, and grease it with some cooking oil so that the toffee does not stick.

2. Blend the berries in a blender or a food processor. Mix the berries with whipping cream, granulated sugar, and syrup in a wide saucepan with a thick bottom.

3. Bring to a boil, then simmer over medium heat until the thermometer shows 252°F (122°C). Check the consistency with the cold water caramel test. Stir regularly. Pour the batter into the pan and allow to solidify.

4. Cut the toffee into square pieces and store at room temperature.

Nougat

Homemade nougat is easier to make than you may think. Use this nougat as filling for the Mozart almond chocolates, or cut into pieces and enjoy as is.

❋ **7 oz (200 g) hazelnuts**
⅗ **cup (90 g) powdered sugar**
7 oz (200 g) dark chocolate

1. Spread the nuts in a baking dish and roast them lightly in the center of the oven at 400°F (200°C) for 5–10 minutes. Stir occasionally and remove the nuts from the oven when they start to give off a lovely aroma and have acquired a beautiful color. Rub them to remove the loose skins.

2. Mix the warm nuts with about a quarter of the powdered sugar in a food processor until the mixture is warm and almost liquid. This takes approximately 5–10 minutes.

3. Gently melt the chocolate in the microwave or in a hot-water bath.

4. Add the chocolate and the remaining powdered sugar in the food processor and mix on a fast speed until everything is thoroughly blended.

5. Pour the nougat into a bowl if you are going to use it for Mozart almond chocolates. Allow it to cool and solidify in the refrigerator for about 1 hour, until the nougat is easy to work with. If it becomes too cold and crumbly, you will need to knead it until it becomes softer.

Almond Paste

Homemade almond paste is easy to make and much tastier than the store-bought kind. This recipe contains raw egg whites, so be sure to use salmonella-controlled eggs.

❋ **about 1⅓ cups (200 g) sweet amonds**   ⅗ **cup (135 g) granulated sugar**
2–3 bitter almonds, or a few drops of   **less than 1 egg white**
   bitter almond extract

1. Scald and peel the sweet and the bitter almonds and chop them finely with the sugar.

2. Add a little bit of egg white in stages, until it all comes together in a thick mass. Add the bitter almond extract if you are using it instead of the bitter almonds.

3. Shape into a ball and cover in plastic wrap. Store the almond paste in the refrigerator until you are ready to use it. It lasts for about two weeks in the refrigerator.

PEELING THE ALMONDS

Measure out the almonds and place them in a heatproof bowl. Pour boiling water over them and leave them in the water for 1–2 minutes. Drain and let the almonds cool until you can handle them. Squeeze the almonds so that they slip out of the shells.

Mozart Almond Chocolates

Homemade marzipan and nougat make Mozart almond chocolates extra special. However, if you want to save time, you can use store-bought marzipan and nougat.

 about 25 pieces

about 1 cup (250 g) homemade
    nougat
1 batch (about 375 g) homemade
    almond paste
about 8.8 oz (250 g) dark chocolate

1. Roll the nougat into balls that are slightly smaller than marbles.

2. Cover the balls with marzipan and reshape into a ball.

3. Gently melt the chocolate in the microwave or in a hot-water bath. Dip the balls in chocolate using a fork, and place the balls on a tray lined with greaseproof paper or parchment paper. Allow to solidify in the refrigerator and keep the balls cold until they are ready to be served.

Mint Fondants

about 20

For the molds and the "kisses"
about 2.5 oz (75 g) dark
    chocolate

Mint Cream
⅘ cup (120 g) powdered sugar
1–1½ tbsp milk
1–2 drops peppermint extract

1. Gently melt the chocolate in the microwave or in a hot-water bath. Brush the interior of the toffee molds or ice chocolate molds with a layer of chocolate. Allow the molds to solidify in the refrigerator for about 20 minutes and then brush the edges with an additional layer of melted chocolate. Sometimes one coat is enough if you make it thick and cover the entire mold.

2. Allow to solidify for at least 20 minutes, and then peel off the aluminum or paper mold from the chocolate.

3. Stir a little bit of milk at a time into the powdered sugar, until you have a fairly thick batter. Add the peppermint extract and taste to make sure that you have enough peppermint flavor.

4. Pipe or spoon mint cream into each chocolate shell. Allow to solidify in the refrigerator for a little while. Then pipe a little bit of melted chocolate onto each praline. Keep these delicious treats in the refrigerator until you want to serve them.

Glögg Truffles

Easy to make, yet impressive and delicious. If you make a double batch, you have a great little gift to bring to all those holiday parties. Glögg wine is a spiced fortified wine, usually served hot or warm, that you can find in some wineries and liquor stores. You can make it yourself by mixing red wine, brandy, orange peel, cloves, and cardamom. It can be replaced with rum, brandy, or any liquor that suits your fancy.

❋ *about 20 pieces*

about 7 oz (200 g) dark chocolate
⅖ cup (100 ml) whipping cream
2 tbsp (25 g) butter
1 tsp honey
2 tbsp of fortified glögg (mulled wine)

cocoa for dipping

1. Place plastic wrap on a 4.5 x 7 inch (12 x 18 cm) dish. Chop the chocolate finely.

2. Bring whipping cream, butter, and honey to a boil. Remove the pan from the heat and quickly add the chocolate. Mix with a hand blender until you have a smooth truffle ganache. Pour the mulled wine into the batter and mix. Pour the truffle mixture into the dish and allow to solidify in the refrigerator for at least 3–4 hours.

3. Take out the truffle from the mold and cut into smaller pieces. To keep truffle ganache from sticking to the knife, you can rinse the knife in hot water and dry it off in between each cut. Allow to solidify in the refrigerator for about 10 minutes.

4. Dip the truffles in cocoa and refrigerate until serving.

WHAT KIND OF CHOCOLATE SHOULD I USE?

Choose whatever chocolate you like. Nowadays, there are lots of different kinds of chocolate in the supermarket. If you prefer a mild and cheap chocolate, use that, or if you like more expensive 70% cocoa chocolate, buy that. Preferably, buy fair trade chocolate.

Gingerbread Chocolate

Delicious candy that you can make in the blink of an eye.

❄ *10–15 pieces*

about 5.3 oz (150 g) dark chocolate
about ⅓ cup (75 g) dried fruit, like
    figs, apricots, or raisins
about 10 gingerbread cookies

1. Melt the chocolate gently in a hot-water bath or in the microwave.
2. Chop or cut the dried fruit into small pieces. Break the gingerbread cookies into small pieces, and stir the dried fruit and the cookie pieces into the chocolate. Mix well until all the pieces are covered with chocolate. Place a dollop of the candy mixture into small paper molds. Store in the refrigerator so that the chocolate solidifies, and keep cold until serving.

Filled Dates

Dip the dates in dark chocolate to make them extra luxurious.

❄ *20 pieces*

20 dried dates
about ⅖ cup (100 g)
    almond paste

1. Cut the dates lengthwise and pick out the core.
2. Shape the almond paste into oblong pieces and put it in the dates. Store in a cool place.

CHOCOLATE IN THE REFRIGERATOR?!

Contrary to what everyone says, I think the refrigerator is the best place to store homemade chocolates, preferably in a jar with a tight-fitting lid. This way they last longer and the surface remains smooth, but it is preferable to remove the pralines from the refrigerator 15–20 minutes before serving them for better taste and texture. You can keep store-bought chocolate bars and chocolates at room temperature.

Ginger Truffle Bars

Place the truffle bars on a beautiful plate along with a knife, so that your guests can cut as much as they want to have with their coffee. Wrap these treats in cellophane, and they'll make a lovely little gift.

❋ *about 15 pieces*

Truffles
about 10.5 oz (300 g) dark chocolate
⅘ cup (200 ml) whipping cream
2 tbsp (25 g) butter
1 tbsp honey
0.75–1 oz (20–30 g) grated fresh ginger
   (about the size of a ping pong ball)

Glaze
about 8.8 oz (250 g) dark chocolate for
   dipping
about 1.7 oz (50 g) white chocolate for
   decoration

1. Cover a dish that is about 4.5 x 7 inches (12 x 18) with plastic wrap.

2. Break the chocolate into small pieces and melt all the ingredients for the truffle on the lowest heat in a saucepan. Stir occasionally and remove the pan from the heat when the truffle blend is smooth and shiny.

3. Pour the truffle mixture into the dish, even out the surface, and allow to solidify in the refrigerator for at least 3–4 hours.

4. Take out the truffle from the mold and cut it into sticks. To keep truffle ganache from getting stuck to the knife, it's best to wash the knife in hot water and dry it with paper towels each time after cutting the truffle. Allow the truffle bars to solidify in the refrigerator for about 10 minutes.

5. Break the dark chocolate for dipping into small pieces and melt it gently in the microwave or in a hot-water bath.

6. Dip the truffle bars in dark chocolate and place them on a tray lined with greaseproof paper.

7. Melt the white chocolate and use it to decorate the sticks. Place them in the refrigerator to solidify, and store in a tightly-sealed jar in the refrigerator. These treats are good for at least three weeks.

Milk Chocolate Truffles

I never get tired of these truffles! With a soft and creamy interior and a crispy shell, they are perfect for all milk chocolate lovers.
Measure and weigh all the ingredients for the truffle carefully to get the right consistency.

❄ *about 25 pieces*

Truffles
about 8.8 oz (250 g) milk
    chocolate
²/₅ cup (100 ml) whipping
    cream
1 tsp honey
2 tbsp (25 g) butter

Decorating
⅘ cup (125 g) chopped hazelnuts
about 7 oz (200 g) milk chocolate

1. Break the chocolate for the truffles into small pieces.

2. Put the whipping cream, honey, and butter in a saucepan. Add the chocolate and melt the ingredients at low heat on the stove. Stir occasionally and remove the pot from the heat when the truffle mixture is smooth and shiny.

3. Let the truffle cool slightly and then solidify in the refrigerator for at least 4 hours. You can also place the truffle in the freezer to make it firmer and easier to handle.

4. Spread the nuts in a baking dish and roast them in the middle of the oven at 450°F (225°C) for 8–10 minutes, or until they become golden brown and smell good. Keep an eye on them so they do not burn, and stir occasionally. Allow them to cool and rub off the loose peels.

5. Roll the truffle into balls. Dry your hands well with paper towels in between each ball so that it's easier to shape them. Let the truffle balls set in the freezer for about 20 minutes until they are firm enough to dip in chocolate.

6. Chop the nuts, and melt the chocolate. Dip the balls in the chocolate, and then in the chopped nuts. Allow the balls to solidify and store in the refrigerator.

Marzipan Figures

You can make beautiful Santas, elves, and other Christmas figures by coloring marzipan with food coloring and molding it into desired shapes.

If you grease your hands with some cooking oil, it will be easier to work with the marzipan, and the figures will have a smoother and shinier surface.

For the most part, the figurine parts will attach to each other easily on their own. However, if you really want to make sure they stick, you can use egg whites.

You can buy black food coloring for the eyes in craft stores, or you can use melted chocolate or licorice sprinkles.

Cookies

Ronneby Gingerbread Cookies

Flavorful and crisp gingerbread cookies origiated and were recorded as early as 1879, in CE Hagdahl's kokbok (CE Hagdahl's Cookbook). Hagdahl himself had received the recipe from "an amateur, who has at his disposal the best resources." I have embraced the slightly more modern version of the recipe from the book Goda pepparkakor och annat got *(Delicious Gingerbread Cookies and Other Treats) from 1952, and the frosting is new also. The dough should be stored overnight, preferably longer.*

❋ *about 250*

Dough
1⅓ cups (270 g) granulated
     sugar
⅘ cup (280 g) maple syrup
⅖ cup (100 ml) strong coffee
4 tsp ground cinnamon
1½ tbsp ground ginger
1½ tsp ground cloves
1⅓ cups (300 g) butter
finely grated zest of 1 lemon
6⅓ cups (900 g) flour
1 tbsp baking soda

Icing
1 egg white
about 1⅓ cups (200 g) powdered sugar
1 tsp vinegar
red and green food coloring

optional: silver dragees for decoration

1. Mix sugar, syrup, coffee, and spices in a saucepan and bring to a boil. Pour the hot mixture over the butter in a large bowl. Stir until the butter has dissolved and continue stirring occasionally, until the batter has cooled and has a creamy texture.

2. Add the grated lemon zest.

3. Mix flour and baking soda and add to the butter batter. Work into a dough and knead until smooth on a floured surface or in a food processor. Wrap in plastic wrap and refrigerate overnight.

4. Roll the dough, a little bit at a time, on a floured surface and cut the cookies into desired shapes. Place them sparsely on trays covered with parchment paper, and bake in the middle of the oven at 400°F (200°C) for 8–10 minutes. Allow to cool.

5. Put the egg white for the icing in a clean, dry bowl, preferably stainless steel. Beat to a stiff foam with an electric whisk.

6. Sift most of the powdered sugar into the egg white and add the vinegar. Continue whisking until the icing is thick, fluffy, and glossy. If needed, add more powdered sugar and whisk until stiff peaks form.

7. Mix icing with a few drops of food coloring, and pipe the icing onto the cookies. Decorate with silver balls.

TIPS!

✽ *This is a batch big enough to share with friends and family.*

✽ *You can store the dough for several weeks in the refrigerator if you wrap it in plastic wrap.*

Gingerbread Sticks

Cute little gingerbread sticks perfect to serve with drinks at your Christmas cocktail party.

about 80 sticks

**about half a batch of Ronneby gingerbread cookies,
or 1 packet of store-bought gingerbread dough
1 egg for brushing
crushed loaf sugar**

1. Roll out a piece of the dough on parchment paper until it is about 6 inches (15 cm) long (the length of the sticks) and 0.2 of an inch (5 mm) thick. If you place a damp cloth underneath the paper, it won't slide when you roll the dough.

2. Brush a thin layer of the beaten egg over the dough and generously sprinkle with crushed loaf sugar.

3. Cut the dough into sticks that are about 0.2 inches (5mm) wide, and part them with a knife so that they are a bit separated on the baking sheet. Repeat with the remaining dough.

4. Bake in the middle of the oven at 400°F (200°C) for about 8–10 minutes or until the sticks are golden brown.

Gingerbread House

Building a gingerbread house is a fun project for Christmas, but expect it to be a bit time-consuming. Don't try to squeeze it into your schedule if you are already stressed about work, holiday parties, and Christmas shopping.

Instead of using burning-hot caramel to glue the house parts together, you can use baking chocolate. In other words, you can use chocolate that may not be very tasty, but that solidifies quickly at room temperature. It doesn't contain enough cocoa butter to be called chocolate.

House
3–4 packets (each containing 17.5 oz/500 grams)
    store-bought gingerbread dough
about 7 oz (200 g) royal icing or
    milk chocolate to piece together the house
gelatin leaves for the windows
candy, marzipan figures, and cotton candy

Icing
2 egg whites
2–2½ cups (about 350 g) powdered
    sugar
1 tsp vinegar

optional: food coloring

1. Trace the house templates on pages 92–94.

2. Roll out the dough on a lightly floured surface until it is 0.08–0.1 inches (2–3 mm) thick. Place the templates on top of the dough and cut along the lines. Also cut a bottom plate that is about 12 x 14 inches (30 x 35 cm). Place the house parts on baking trays that have been lined with parchment paper and cut out the windows.

3. Bake in the middle of the oven at 400°F (200°C) for about 10 minutes or until the pieces are golden brown. After taking them out, allow them to cool completely.

4. If using chocolate for gluing, melt it gently in the microwave or in a hot-water bath and allow to cool slightly. If it solidifies while it cools, you can reheat it.

5. Attach the gelatin leaves on the inside of the windows with some royal icing or melted chocolate.

6. Place the bottom plate on a tray. Put the walls together with a generous amount of royal icing or chocolate as an adhesive, and stick them onto the base. Hold the pieces together until the icing or chocolate has solidified.

7. Attach the roof on top of the house, and then add the chimney and the door.

8. Prepare the icing in the same way as shown on page 30, directions 5–7. Decorate the house with lots of icing and candy.

TIPS!

❋ *You can roll out the gingerbread dough directly on the baking paper. Place a damp cloth underneath the paper to prevent it from sliding. Cut out the house parts with a little bit of space between them, then drag the baking paper onto a baking tray.*

❋ *If the house parts change shape during the baking process, you can file them gently on a fine grater.*

❋ *Store the gingerbread house in a dry place. Moisture can cause it to collapse.*

Gingerbread Bowl

A homemade gingerbread bowl is the cutest way to serve Christmas candy, fruits, or nuts.

❋

**1 packet of store-bought gingerbread dough,
or half a batch of the batter for the
Ronneby gingerbread cookies
1 batch of the icing for the Ronneby gingerbread cookies**

Use the templates on page 95.

For the gingerbread bowl shells, use the same instructions as for the gingerbread house on page 34.

❋

We have been enjoying gingerbread cookies since the Middle Ages, and they used to be flavored with actual pepper. The cookies were compared to medicine, because spices such as pepper, ginger, and cloves were used to cure cholera, melancholia, tooth ache, and poor eyesight. Gingerbread cookies used to be so spicy that we probably wouldn't be able to eat them by today's standards. The gingerbread cookie is said to come from Germany, where they used to be called "cakes of life."

Cinnamon Cookies

Generously big and scrumptious cookies!

✳ *about 15 cookies*

7 tbsp (100 g) butter
⅗ cup (120 g) brown sugar
1 egg
⅘ cup (120 g) flour
⅘ cup (125 g) oats
1 tsp baking powder

1 tsp ground ginger
1 tsp ground cinnamon
about 2.6 oz (75 g) dark chocolate
⅔ cup (125 g) hazelnuts, preferably
 roasted and peeled
⅔ cup (about 50 g) dried cranberries

1. Melt the butter and stir in the brown sugar.

2. Add the egg, flour, oats, baking powder, and spices, and mix to make a thick batter.

3. Chop the chocolate coarsely and work into the dough along with the hazelnuts and cranberries.

4. Shape the dough into balls and flatten them slightly. Spread them out on trays covered with parchment paper. The cookies will expand a lot during the baking process.

5. Bake in the middle of the oven at 350°F (175°C) for 10–12 minutes, or until the cookies turn golden brown.

TIP!

If you want to make fun and thoughtful gifts, pour the batter into beautiful jars or containers. Then the receivers can bake the cookies whenever they want to fill their kitchens with the lovely aroma of freshly-baked cookies.

Currant Cookies

Modest in appearance, but divine in taste. Fill a jar with these delicious treats so that you can nibble on them throughout the holiday season. Currants resemble raisins but are smaller, and they are available in the baking section in most supermarkets.

 60–70 small cookies

10 tbsp (150 g) butter
1⅓ cups (about 200 g) rolled oats
⅗ cup (180 g) flour
⅗ cup (135 g) granulated sugar
1½ tsp baking powder
1 tsp ground cinnamon
½ tsp ground cloves
⅖ cup (100 ml) milk
1⅓ cups (about 200 g) currants

1. Melt the butter in a saucepan on the stove or in a bowl in the microwave.

2. Stir all the dry ingredients into the butter, add the milk, and work together to form a thick batter. Stir the currants into the batter and mix well.

3. Spoon small portions of dough onto baking trays lined with parchment paper. Bake in the center of the oven at 400°F (200°C) for just under 8 minutes. Allow to cool.

Cinnamon Hearts

··

Crisp and scrumptious hearts that almost melt in your mouth. You can halve the recipe if you do not want to make quite as many cookies.

❋ *50–60 Cookies*

2 cups (300 g) flour
⅖ cup (90 g) granulated sugar
2 pinches of salt
about ⅘ cup (200 g) cold butter
2 egg yolks

granulated sugar and cinnamon for decoration

1. Place all the ingredients for the cookies in a food processor and pulse quickly into a dough. You can also form the dough by hand.

2. Allow the dough to rest in the refrigerator for at least 30 minutes. If it becomes too hard, just knead it on a work surface until it softens again.

3. Roll out the dough on a floured surface until it is about 0.08 inches (2 mm) thick. Use a cookie cutter to cut out hearts and spread the cookies sparsely on trays covered with parchment paper.

4. Bake the cookies in the middle of the oven at 400°F (200°C) for 6–7 minutes. Mix the sugar with the cinnamon and sprinkle cinnamon sugar over the cookies as soon as they come out of the oven. Allow to cool.

LINGONBERRY COOKIES!

You can modify the dough for the cinnamon hearts to create a variety of different cookies. Make delicious lingonberry cookies by rolling the dough into circles with the same diameter as a dollar coin. Place them in the refrigerator for about 30 minutes, and then cut them into slices that are 0.1 inch (3 mm) thick. Place the slices on a tray covered with parchment paper, make a little indentation in the center of each cookie, and fill the hole with a dollop of lingonberry jam. Bake in the center of the oven at 400°F (200°C) for about 8 minutes.

Candy Cane Cookies

Double the recipe as these cookies are likely to be gone in no time!

10–12 large cookies

5.3 oz (150 g) dark chocolate
7 tbsp (100 g) butter
⅗ cup (about 120 g) brown sugar
1 egg
⅘ cup (120 g) flour
⅗ cup (95 g) rolled oats
1 tsp baking powder
about ⅖ cup (100 g) crushed candy canes or peppermint sticks

optional: a few drops of peppermint extract

1. Melt the chocolate with the butter in the microwave or in a saucepan over low heat. Add brown sugar and stir.

2. Add the egg, flour, oatmeal, and baking powder, and mix to make a thick batter. Add a few drops of peppermint extract if you want an extra minty flavor.

3. Crush the candy canes and work two-thirds of the canes into the batter.

4. Shape the batter into fairly large balls, flatten them, and spread them sparsely on trays covered with parchment paper. The cookies will expand quite a bit during the baking process.

5. Bake in the center of the oven at 350°F (175°C) for 10–12 minutes. Sprinkle the crushed candy canes on the cookies immediately after baking.

Ginger Cake

Candles aren't only for birthday cakes; they also look beautiful on a soft and moist gingerbread cake.

✳

Cake

⅓ cup (75 g) butter
1 cup (150 g) flour
1½ tsp baking powder
1 tbsp gingerbread spice, or the equivalent
   amount of ground cinnamon, cardamom, cloves, and ginger
3 eggs
⅘ cup (180 g) granulated sugar
⅗ cup (about 150 ml) sour cream, milk, or soured milk
butter and breadcrumbs for the baking dish

Icing

7 oz (200 g) cream cheese
2 tbsp lingonberry or cranberry jam

1. Butter and bread a loaf pan that holds about 1½ quarts (1½ l).

2. Melt the butter for the cake.

3. Mix flour, baking powder, and gingerbread spices.

4. Beat eggs and sugar with an electric mixer until fluffy.

5. Sift flour mixture a little bit at a time into the butter and sour cream, and whisk gently into a smooth batter with a hand whisk.

6. Pour the batter into the loaf pan and bake in the lower part of the oven at 350°F (175°C) for 45–50 minutes. Turn the cake upside down onto parchment paper or a cooling rack to allow it to cool for a few minutes, and then loosen it from the mold. Let the cake cool completely.

7. Mix the cream cheese with lingonberry jam. Spread the glaze over the gingerbread cake, and let the cake stand in a cool place until it's ready to be served.

Gingerbread Cupcakes

These muffins create a wonderfully spicy aroma in the kitchen!

❄ *about 15 pieces*

Muffins
7 tbsp (100 g) butter
3 eggs
⅘ cup (180 g) granulated sugar
1 cup (150 g) flour
1 tsp baking powder
1 pinch salt
1 tbsp ground gingerbread spice
⅗ cup (150 ml) milk

Frosting
⅓ cup (35 g) powdered sugar
2 tbsp lemon juice
a few drops of red food coloring
10.5 oz (300 g) cream cheese
⅖ cup (100 ml) whipping cream

optional: snowflake sprinkles for decoration

1. Melt the butter slowly in a saucepan or in a bowl in the microwave.

2. Beat the eggs with the sugar in a bowl.

3. Mix flour, baking powder, salt, and gingerbread spice and stir into the egg mixture together with the milk. Add the melted butter and stir.

4. Pour the batter into cupcake cups or a lined cupcake pan and bake at 350°F (175°C) in the middle of the oven for about 20–25 minutes. Allow to cool.

5. To make the frosting, add the powdered sugar, lemon juice, and food coloring to the cream cheese and whisk. Add the whipping cream, little by little, and whisk to make a fluffy frosting.

6. Pipe or spread the icing on top of the muffins and decorate with sprinkles if you are using them.

TIP!
Around Christmastime, well-stocked department stores usually sell muffin pans that are shaped like gingerbread men. They are great when you want to bake muffin figures; just make sure to butter and bread the molds generously. Otherwise follow the same recipe.

Saffron Cake with Lemon

This batch is enough to fill a regular-sized cake pan, but I have used a slightly larger cake pan for the cake in the photo, which requires nearly a double batch.

⅓ cup (75 g) butter
1⅓ cups (180 g) flour
2 tsp baking powder
¼ g saffron
⅘ cup (180 g) granulated sugar
3 eggs
finely grated zest of 1 lemon
⅕ cup (50 ml) freshly squeezed lemon juice
⅖ cup (100 ml) milk

butter and breadcrumbs for the cake pan

1. Melt the butter.

2. Mix flour and baking powder.

3. Crush the saffron with a little bit of sugar to pulverize it finely.

4. Use an electric mixer to beat eggs, sugar, and saffron sugar until fluffy. Add the grated lemon zest towards the end and whisk.

5. Sift the flour mixture, a little bit at a time, into the batter. Add the butter, lemon juice, and milk, and whisk gently until smooth with a hand whisk.

6. Butter a cake pan that holds at least 1½ q/1½ l and sprinkle it with breadcrumbs.

7. Pour the batter into the cake pan and bake at the bottom of the oven at 350°F (175°C) for about 40 minutes. Turn the cake upsidedown onto parchment paper or a wire rack, wait a few minutes, and loosen the cake from the mold. Allow to cool.

Almond Tartlets

•••

To create a really cozy Christmas just like grandmother's, these almond tartlets are a must!
The cookies are deliciously crisp and are filled with jam and fluffy whipped cream.

You will need tartlet molds, which can be purchased at the grocery store or at the nearest flea market.

❋ *about 35 pieces*

⅘ cup (125 g) almonds, or ground almonds
¾ cup (175 g) butter
⅗ cup (135 g) granulated sugar
1 egg
1¾ cups (240 g) flour

optional: a few drops of bitter almond extract

flour for the molds
whipped cream and jam to serve

1. Scald, peel, and grind the almonds (you can read about how to scald almonds on page 15). If you don't have an almond grinder, you can chop them finely in a food processor.

2. Mix soft butter with sugar. Add the ground almonds, one egg, flour, and possibly a few drops of bitter almond extract. Quickly work into a dough. Shape the dough into a log, wrap in plastic wrap, and place in the refrigerator for at least 1 hour.

3. Sprinkle the molds with a little bit of flour. Cut the dough log into slices and place in the molds. Smooth the edges, and place the molds on a tray.

4. Bake in middle of oven at 400°F (200°C) for about 8 minutes or until golden brown. Allow to cool for a few minutes and then loosen the almond tartlets from the molds. It makes it easier if you squeeze gently on the aluminum mold edges so they slide out. Serve with whipped cream and jam.

Toffee Brownies

When the photographer, Ulrika Pousette, tasted these brownies during the shoot for this book, she was completely speechless. Eventually, she managed to say: "These are just THE most delicious brownies!" And I don't disagree.

❋ *12 large pieces*

about 8.8 oz (250 g) dark chocolate, preferably 70% cocoa
about 1 cup (250 g) butter
⅘ cup (160 g) brown sugar
3 eggs
1 egg yolk
⅖ cup (60 g) flour
⅗ cup (60 g) cocoa
½ tsp baking powder
1 pinch salt
about 15 toffee candies (see page 8), roughly chopped

1. Line a baking dish, about 8 x 10 inches (20 x 26 cm), with parchment paper.

2. Melt about 7 oz (200 g) of chocolate in a hot-water bath or in the microwave and let it cool for a bit. Chop the rest of the chocolate coarsely.

3. Beat the butter and brown sugar with an electric mixer until soft and fluffy.

4. Add the eggs, and the yolk one at a time, and whisk well in between each. Add the melted chocolate into the batter and stir.

5. Combine flour, cocoa, baking powder, and salt, and sift into the batter. Gently mix and add the chopped chocolate and the toffee.

6. Pour the batter into the baking dish and smooth out the surface. Bake in the center of the oven at 350°F (175°C) for about 30 minutes. Check the batter with a stick, it should be stiff and not runny, but the cake should not be completely dry.

7. Allow the cake to cool and cut it into pieces.

Fruit Cake

Absolutely delicious with a cup of tea! Snuggle up with a cozy blanket and enjoy the winter cold outside.

about 1⅓ cups (200 g) dried fruit, like figs, apple rings, apricots, and raisins
2 tbsp rum or brandy
grated zest and juice of 1 orange
¾ cup (175 g) butter
⅗ cup (135 g) sugar
3 eggs
1⅓ cups (180 g) flour
2 tsp baking powder
about 1⅓ cups (150 g) nuts, like walnuts and hazelnuts
1 grated apple
butter and breadcrumbs for the baking pan

1. Butter and bread a cake pan that holds at least 1½ quarts (1½ l).

2. Chop the dried fruit coarsely, and mix with rum or brandy and zest and juice from the orange. Allow to sit for a while.

3. Stir softened butter with sugar. Add in one egg at a time and stir.

4. Mix flour with baking powder and stir into the butter mixture. Mix until it thickens.

5. Chop the nuts coarsely and stir into the mixture along with the grated apple. Add the dried fruit with the orange and rum blend.

6. Pour the batter into the pan and bake at the bottom of the oven at 350°F (175°C) for about 65 minutes. Cover the top of the cake if it starts to get too much color.

7. Invert the cake onto a wire rack, allow to cool for a few minutes, and then remove the mold. You can store the cake for at least one week at room temperature.

Desserts

Rice Pudding Pie

Next time you make rice pudding, make a big batch so that you have enough to make this delicious pie. It may not look like much, but it's surprisingly good. I got the idea from the Italian pie, torta di riso, but I think it's just as good on a traditional Christmas table.

✳

Pie Dough
1⅓ cups (180 g) flour
1½ tbsp granulated sugar
about 9 tbsp (125 g) cold butter

Filling
⅓ cup (75 g) butter
2 eggs
⅓ cup (75 g) granulated sugar
about 1¾ cups (500 g) rice pudding, homemade or bought
finely grated zest of 1 orange
finely grated zest of 1 lemon

1. Combine flour and sugar for the pastry dough. Add the butter in pieces and work together with your fingertips or in a food processor.

2. Press the dough into a pie dish about 9.5 inches (24 cm) in diameter, and smooth out the edges with a knife. Place the pie dish in the refrigerator for at least 30 minutes.

3. Remove the pie shell from the refrigerator and prick holes in it with a fork. Bake in the middle of the oven at 400°F (200°C) for 10–12 minutes, or until the dough starts to get some color.

4. Melt the butter for the filling. Lightly beat the eggs and two-thirds of the sugar with a fork. Stir the egg mixture into the pudding with the butter and the grated lemon zest. Spread the batter in the pie shell and sprinkle with the remaining sugar.

5. Bake in the middle of the oven at 400°F (200°C) for about 20 minutes until the top is golden brown. Serve the pie warm or cold with whipped cream and jam.

Fig Pie

So beautiful and delectable! Enjoy this pie warm with a dollop of whipped cream for dessert, or cool with a cup of coffee.

Pie dough
1⅓ cups (180 g) flour
1½ tbsp granulated sugar
about 9 tbsp (125 g) cold butter

Filling
about 1 cup (100 g) walnut kernels
7 tbsp (100 g) unsalted butter
⅖ cup (90 g) granulated sugar
1 tbsp vanilla sugar
2 eggs
⅕ cup (50 ml) milk
6 fresh figs

optional: fresh rosemary for decoration

1. Combine flour and powdered sugar for the pastry. Add the butter in pieces and work into a dough with your fingertips or a food processor. Press the dough into a pie dish, preferably a square shape that is about 8.5 x 8.5 inches (22 x 22 cm). Place in the refrigerator for at least 30 minutes.

2. Prepare the filling. Chop the walnuts finely in a food processor. Add the butter, granulated sugar, and vanilla sugar, and mix until you have a smooth batter.

3. Add the eggs and milk, and mix briefly.

4. Remove the pie shell from the refrigerator and use a fork to prick holes in the dough. Bake in the middle of the oven at 400°F (200°C) for 10–12 minutes until the dough starts to get some color.

5. Spread walnut filling in the pie shell. Halve the figs and place them in the pie shell. Bake for another 30–35 minutes at 350°F (175°C). Allow to cool slightly.

Christmas Pudding

Believe it or not, this Christmas pudding recipe has been simplified, although it may look long and complicated. However, this pudding is absolutely delicious, and you can prepare it weeks ahead if you want to.

❄ *14–16 portions*

about 3 cups (500 g) mixed dried fruit,
   such as apple rings, prunes,
   figs, raisins, apricots, and cranberries
7 tbsp (100 g) butter
juice and zest of 1 lemon
juice and zest of 1 orange
⅗ cup (120 g) brown sugar
2 tbsp brandy

3 tbsp port wine, sherry, or mulled wine
⅗ cup (90 g) flour
½ tsp each of ground ginger,
   ground nutmeg, and ground cinnamon
1 apple, peeled and grated
2 eggs, lightly beaten
3.5 oz (100 g) white bread, sliced with
   crusts removed

1. Butter two small oven dishes or one large baking pan for pudding, soufflé, or cakes.

2. Chop the dried fruit quite finely, or pulse it in the food processor.

3. Mix the chopped fruit in a saucepan with butter, juice, zest of the lemon and orange, brown sugar, brandy, and port wine. Bring to a boil and simmer on low heat for a few minutes. Remove the pan from the heat and allow the mixture to cool slightly.

4. Mix the flour with the spices and stir into the fruit mixture along with the apple and eggs.

5. Crumble the bread or mix it in a food processor and then add it to the batter. Pour the batter into the baking pans, leaving less than half an inch (1 cm) to the top edge, and smooth the surface. Cut a piece of parchment paper and place it on top of the batter. Cover the top with aluminum foil.

6. Fill a roasting pan halfway with hot water. Place the dish in the water bath and bake in the lower part of the oven at 300°F (150°C) for 3 hours. Add water if it evaporates.

7. Lift the mold out of the water bath and turn the pudding upside-down onto a sheet of parchment paper. Wait for a few minutes before you release the pudding from the mold. Allow to cool slightly and serve with lightly whipped cream. If you aren't serving the pudding right away, you can reheat it in the microwave.

Glögg Cheesecake

This glögg-flavored cheesecake is creamy and refreshing, yet sweet and savory. You can prepare this cake a few days in advance, which makes it the perfect stress-free dessert after Christmas dinner.

❋

Crust
7 oz (200 g) gingerbread cookies
⅓ cup (75 g) butter

Filling
3 eggs
⅖ cup (90 g) granulated sugar
about 2 cups (500 g) cream cheese
⅘ cup (1 can/about 184 g) light
 crème fraiche or sour cream
⅖ cup (100 ml) non-alcoholic
 glögg (mulled wine)

Glögg wine jelly
3 gelatin leaves
⅘ cup (200 ml) non-alcoholic
 glögg (mulled wine)

optional: cinnamon sticks
 and fresh figs to garnish
 the cake

1. Dress the bottom of a springform pan, with a removable rim about 8.5 inches (22 cm) in diameter, with parchment paper.

2. Crumble the cookies quite finely in a mortar or chop them in a food processor. Melt the butter and stir it into the cookie crumbs. Mix into a crumbly mass and press an even layer of the cookie dough into the bottom of the pan. Bake the bottom in the middle of the oven at 350°F (175°C) for about 10 minutes.

3. Beat the eggs lightly with the sugar. Beat the cream cheese and the crème fraiche or sour cream into the egg batter. Whisk to a smooth, loose paste and stir the mulled wine into the batter.

4. Pour the batter into the pan and bake at the bottom of the oven at 350°F (175°C) for 30–35 minutes. The cake should still be a little bit loose in the middle. It will solidify and become just the right creamy texture when it has cooled. Allow the cake to cool completely at room temperature and then chill it in the refrigerator. Sometimes the cake tends to crack a little bit, but that is normal and you can always even it out.

5. Soak the gelatin in cold water for a few minutes. Gently heat the mulled wine in the microwave or in a small saucepan. Shake off any excess water from the gelatin leaves and add them to the warm mulled wine to dissolve. Allow the solution to cool for a few minutes before you carefully pour a thin layer over the cheesecake. Allow to solidify in the refrigerator.

6. Loosen the cake from the pan edge with a small knife, remove the bottom of the springform pan, and remove the parchment paper from the cake. Optionally, decorate the cake with cinnamon sticks and fresh figs.

Chocolate Pastries with Blood Orange Cream

••

This fancy pastry is suitable during Advent, as well as New Year's Eve. This recipe takes quite some time and is great if you want to take on a bit of a challenge. The chocolate spirals are a nice addition, but the dessert will be just as pretty with only kumquats as garnish, or chocolate peeled from a chocolate bar a potato peeler.

❋ *about 10 pastries*

Blood orange cream
2 egg yolks
2 tsp cornstarch
2 tsp granulated sugar
⅖ cup (100 ml) whipping cream
⅓ cup (75 ml) freshly-squeezed
   blood orange juice
   (1–2 oranges needed)

Chocolate mousse
about 7 oz (200 g) dark chocolate
⅗ + ⅗ cup (150 ml + 150 ml)
   whipping cream
1 tbsp honey

Cake
2 eggs
⅖ cup (90 g) granulated sugar
⅕ cup (32 g) potato flour
1½ tbsp cocoa
½ tsp baking powder

granulated sugar to sprinkle over the cake
kumquats and chocolate spirals for decoration
Cointreau or similar citrus liqueur to
   moisten the cake bottom

1. Begin by making the orange cream. Whisk together egg yolks, cornstarch, and granulated sugar in a saucepan. Then add whipping cream and orange juice and whisk. Bring the cream to a boil and simmer gently for a minute or longer, until it thickens. Whisk continuously and remove the pan from heat. Allow to cool a little, before placing it in the refrigerator.

2. Chop the chocolate for the mousse coarsely. Boil half (⅗ cup /150 ml) of the whipping cream together with the honey in a small saucepan. When the cream starts to bubble, remove the pan from the heat and quickly add the chocolate. Stir until the chocolate has dissolved and the mixture is smooth and shiny. Pour the chocolate into a bowl, cover with plastic wrap, and allow it to cool completely at room temperature. It takes about 2 hours.

3. Beat the rest of the whipping cream (⅗ cup/150 ml) lightly, and let it sit at room temperature for about 30 minutes to get a little bit warmer. It's important that the cream isn't too cold when you fold it into the chocolate mixture to make a chocolate mousse.

4. Beat the eggs together with the sugar for the cake.

5. Mix potato flour, cocoa, and baking powder, and sift or gently whisk into the egg batter.

6. Spread an even, thin layer of the batter over a baking sheet lined with parchment paper. Bake in the middle of the oven at 450°F (225°) for about 6 minutes. Don't bake it for too long, or the cake will get a brittle texture. Sprinkle sugar over the top of the cake, place on a baking sheet, and invert so the cake comes out. Remove the parchment paper and let cool.

7. Save about a half-cup of the chocolate batter for garnish, and fold the whipping cream into the remaining chocolate batter. Fold until you have a fluffy mousse, and store it in the refrigerator until it thickens if the mousse is too loose.

8. Cut the cake horizontally into four layers. Spread half of the chocolate mousse over one of the cake bottoms, then place another cake piece on top. Spread blood orange cream over this piece, then add the next cake piece. Spread the remaining chocolate mousse over it, and place the last cake piece on top.

9. Spread most of the chocolate batter that you set aside over the cake, and drizzle or pipe the rest of it in a decorative pattern. If you want to make the glaze a little thinner for decorating the cake, you can heat it up for a few seconds in the microwave.

10. Cut the cake into long, thin pieces. To avoid smearing, it's best to wash the knife in hot water and dry it with a paper towel in between each cut.

11. Decorate with kumquats and chocolate spirals.

Vanilla Ice Cream with Pomegranate and Nougat

This festive dessert fuses sweet and tangy flavors with creamy and crunchy textures in a perfect marriage. Nougatine is a French variation of toffee that is thin and crispy.

❄ *Serves 4*

Nougat
⅖ cup (60 g) peeled almonds
    or almond flakes
⅘ cup (180 g) granulated sugar
½ tbsp butter
1 pinch salt

Serve with
1 pomegranate
about 1½–2 cups (½ l) vanilla ice cream

1. Chop the almonds if you are using whole almonds.

2. Prepare by taking out two sheets of parchment paper and a rolling pin.

3. Put the granulated sugar in a wide saucepan with a thick bottom. Melt the sugar on the stove at a fairly high temperature. Lower the heat when the sugar starts to get some color and caramelize until it's golden brown. Add the butter and salt and stir.

4. Remove the pan from the heat and quickly add the almonds. Pour the caramel over one of the parchment papers and cover with the other sheet of parchment paper. Roll the caramel into a thin sheet. Allow to cool.

5. When you serve this dessert, layer pomegranate seeds with bits of the nougat and scoops of vanilla ice cream.

TIP!
There are many different ways to remove seeds from a pomegranate. Some people smack the halves with a wooden ladle, while others pick the seeds out in a bowl filled with water. I think it's easier to cut the fruit into quarters, then twist them, and pick out the seeds. However, this process is a little bit messy, so make sure that you aren't wearing your brand-new white dress.

Buns and Breads

HOW TO MAKE SUCCULENT SAFFRON BUNS:

✳ *Don't add too much flour to the dough; allow it to be a little bit sticky.*

✳ *Knead the dough thoroughly, preferably for 5–10 minutes by hand, or in a food processor.*

✳ *Allow the dough to rise for at least 40 minutes, but preferably longer. If you want, you can decrease the amount of yeast you use and leave the dough to rise in the refrigerator overnight.*

Saffron Buns "Lucia Cats"

Saffron buns, or Lucia cats, are a must on Christmas Eve. Enjoy them freshly-baked with a cup of coffee or tea, and store any leftovers in the freezer. The "S" shape is most common, but you can make them into any shape you fancy.

❋ *about 35 buns*

Dough
1.8 oz (50 g) fresh yeast
about 7 cups (1,020 g) flour
½ tsp salt
2 cups (500 ml) milk
1 g saffron
⅗ cup (135 g) sugar
8.8 oz (250 g) ricotta cheese
7 tbsp (100 g) unsalted butter
1 egg for brushing
raisins for garnish

1. Crumble the yeast into a large bowl.

2. Measure and mix flour and salt.

3. Heat milk until it's lukewarm.

4. Mix the saffron with some of the sugar and stir into the milk.

5. Pour the milk over the yeast and dissolve it. Add the flour mixture, the remaining sugar, the soft butter, and ricotta cheese. Work into a dough and knead thoroughly, preferably for 5 minutes in a food processor or 10 minutes by hand.

6. Allow the dough to rise, covered, for at least 40 minutes.

7. Divide the dough into about 35 smaller pieces and shape into desired figures. Spread the buns sparsely on trays covered with parchment paper and allow them to rise, covered, for 30–40 minutes.

8. Brush the buns with whisked egg and decorate with raisins. Bake in the center of the oven at 450°F (225°C) for about 6–7 minutes.

Saffron Buns with Apple and Almond Paste

One way to get wonderfully tasty and moist saffron buns is to fill them with lots of flavorful filling and bake them tightly together in a roasting pan. If you have a lot of time on your hands, you don't need lukewarm milk. It takes a bit longer for the dough to rise with cold milk, but the buns will have more flavor.

about 16—18 buns

Dough

0.9 oz (25 g) yeast
3⅗ cups (510 g) flour
1 pinch salt
1 cup (250 ml) milk
½ g saffron
⅕ cup (45 g) granulated sugar
⅓ cup (75 g) butter
1 egg

Filling

⅓ cup (75 g) butter
2 tsp cinnamon
⅓ cup (75 g) almond paste or
    marzipan
1 small apple, about 125 g

1 egg for brushing
crushed loaf sugar for
    sprinkling

1. Crumble the yeast into a large bowl.

2. Mix the flour and salt.

3. Heat the milk until it is lukewarm.

4. Mix the saffron well with some of the sugar and stir into the milk.

5. Pour the milk over the yeast and dissolve it. Add the flour mixture, the remaining sugar, the soft butter, and the egg.

6. Work into a dough and knead thoroughly, preferably for 5 minutes in a food processor or 10 minutes by hand. Allow the dough to rise, covered, for at least 40 minutes.

7. Meanwhile, mix the butter and cinnamon for the filling.

8. Roll out the dough into a rectangle that is about 0.4 of an inch (1 cm) thick. Spread the cinnamon butter over it and grate and sprinkle the almond paste on top.

9. Grate the apple, allow any fluid to drain off, and sprinkle it over the dough. Roll the dough into a roll and cut it into thick slices. Spread the buns a little bit apart in a greased baking dish, about 8 × 12 inches (20 x 30 cm). Allow to rise, covered, for about 40 minutes.

10. Brush the buns with the beaten egg, sprinkle with crushed loaf sugar, and bake in the middle of the oven at 400°F (200°C) for about 20–25 minutes.

Saffron Twists with Orange and Vanilla

....

No one can resist the aroma of freshly-baked saffron buns stuffed with butter, sugar, vanilla, and orange!

Vanilla powder is ground vanilla that is sold in well-stocked supermarkets. If you can't find any, you may replace it with double the amount of vanilla sugar.

❋ *about 16—18 buns*

Dough
1 batch of the dough for the saffron buns with apple and almond paste

Filling
⅓ cup (75 g) butter
⅔ cup (90 g) granulated sugar
1 tsp vanilla powder
finely grated zest from 2 oranges

1 egg for brushing
crushed loaf sugar and chopped hazelnuts to sprinkle over the twists

1. Prepare the dough the same way as for the saffron buns, and allow it to rise, covered, for at least 40 minutes.

2. Meanwhile, mix the butter and sugar for the filling. Add the vanilla powder and grated orange peel.

3. Roll out dough into a long and narrow rectangle, about 0.4 of an inch (1 cm) thick.

4. Spread the filling over the dough. Fold the dough lengthwise. First, fold over one third, then fold over the second third on top of the first.

5. Cut the dough into strips that are about 0.8 of an inch (2 cm) wide. Twist the dough strips into knots and place the buns sparsely on trays covered with parchment paper. Allow to rise, covered, for about 40 minutes.

6. Brush the buns with the beaten egg, and sprinkle with crushed loaf sugar and chopped hazelnuts. Bake in the center of the oven at 450°F (225°C) for about 8 minutes.

Fruit and Nut Bread

This bread is luxurious, moist, tasty, and filled with dried fruit and walnuts. Enjoy it at the Christmas breakfast table, or serve it for lunch or dinner.

To make the bread extra tasty, add less yeast and allow it to rise longer.

❋← *2 loaves*

0.9 oz (25 g) yeast
3⅗ cups (800 ml) buttermilk
about 4¼ cups (600 g) flour
2 cups (275 g) coarse rye flour
½ tsp salt
⅕ cup (70 grams) maple syrup
3 tbsp (50 ml) canola oil or olive oil
about 1½ cups (200 g) dried fruit, such as figs and apples
1⅓ cups (150 g) walnut kernels

butter for the molds

1. Stir the yeast into the cold buttermilk in a large bowl.

2. Add flour, rye flour, salt, syrup, and oil. Stir it into a loose dough and knead it for about 5 minutes. It's easiest to use a food processor because this dough tends to be quite sticky.

3. Chop the dried fruits and walnuts coarsely and add them last.

4. Cover the bowl and allow the dough to rise for 2–3 hours. Place it in a warm place if you're in a hurry; it will speed up the process.

5. Grease two bread pans with butter, each should be able to hold about 1½ quarts (1½ l). Carefully fill the pans with the dough; you can use a spatula or a trowel that you have dipped in water to keep things less messy. Smooth out the top and let the loaves rise for about 1 hour or until the dough has risen a little above the pan's edge.

6. Bake the breads in the bottom of the oven at 400°F (200°C) for about 60 minutes if you use a Teflon baking dish, and about 15–20 minutes longer if you use an older pan that doesn't contain any Teflon. Cover the top of the breads with some parchment paper if they are getting too much color. Take the breads out of the molds and allow them to cool.

Saffron Bread

Saffron is not only suitable as a seasoning for sweet breads; it makes an excellent seasoning for Christmas breads. If you allow the dough to stay quite loose, the bread will turn out moist and delicious. Make sure to use a lot of flour on the baking surface so that it doesn't get too sticky.

❋ *about 15 bread buns*

1 cup (250 ml) milk
0.9 oz (25 g) yeast
1 egg
2 cups (300 g) bread flour
1 cup (180 g) graham flour
1 tsp salt
½ g saffron
1 tsp granulated sugar
⅓ cup (75 g) butter

flour for the work surface

1. Mix milk, yeast, and eggs in a bowl.

2. Measure and mix the flours with the salt.

3. Mix the saffron well with the granulated sugar and stir it into the milk batter.

4. Mix in the flour blend and the soft butter into the milk batter to form a sticky dough. Knead the dough thoroughly, preferably for 5 minutes in a food processor or 10 minutes by hand. Allow the dough to rise for at least 40 minutes, preferably longer.

5. Generously flour the work surface and place the sticky dough on top. Sprinkle flour on top of the dough, and roll it out to a rectangle that is about 0.8 of an inch (2 cm) thick.

6. Cut the dough into square pieces with a spatula or a knife. Spread the pieces sparsely on trays covered with parchment paper, cover with a towel, and allow the dough to rise for 40 minutes.

7. Bake the breads in the center of the oven at 400°F (200°C) for about 15 minutes.

8. You can fill the cooled breads with ham, cheese, spinach leaves, and a dollop of mustard, or any of your favorite toppings.

Poppy Crisp Bread

Thin and luxuriously crisp bread is delicious with a piece of herring, spiced cheese, or ham. Don't fret about making the pieces even; this rustic crisp bread looks gorgeous when it is a little bit asymmetrical. You can break the bread into bite-size pieces after the baking process.

You can find blue poppy seeds at specialty food stores or well-stocked grocery stores, but if you can't get ahold of them, you can use white poppy seeds or sesame seeds.

0.9 oz (25 g) yeast
1 cup (250 ml) lukewarm water
1¾ cups (240 g) wheat flour
⅗ cup (90 g) spelt flour
1½ tsp salt
1 tbsp canola oil or olive oil
⅖ cup (58 g) blue poppy seeds

flour for the baking surface
fine sea salt or sea salt flakes to sprinkle

1. Crumble the yeast into a bowl, add the water, and stir so the yeast dissolves a little bit.

2. Mix the flours with the salt, stir into the water mixture, and add the oil. Stir until you get a rather sticky dough and knead it for a few minutes. Add the poppy seeds. Allow the dough to rise, covered, for 30 minutes.

3. Generously flour the work surface. Divide the dough into 8–10 pieces and roll each piece out as thinly as possible.

4. Place the crisp bread on trays covered with parchment paper and prick holes in the dough with a fork. Sprinkle with some fine sea salt (don't be too generous; it's easy to add too much salt) and bake one tray at time in the middle of the oven at 450°F (225°C). Bake until the breads are evenly golden brown, about 12–15 minutes. Crisp bread is extra tasty when it's thoroughly baked, so make sure to not remove it from the oven too soon. Allow the breads to cool, and store them in a dry place.

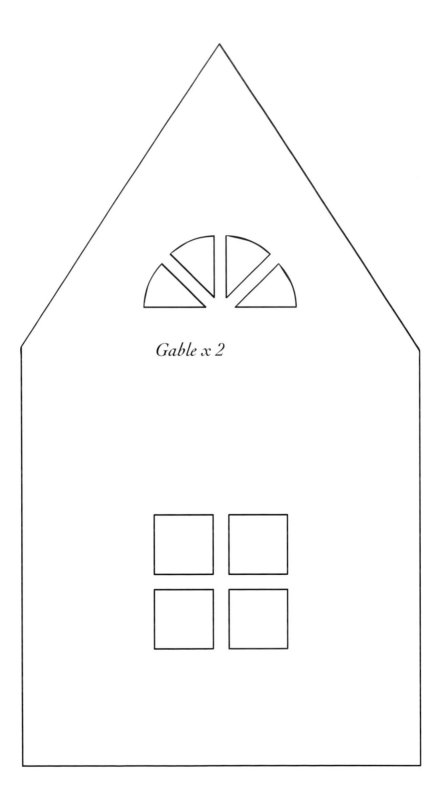

Gable x 2

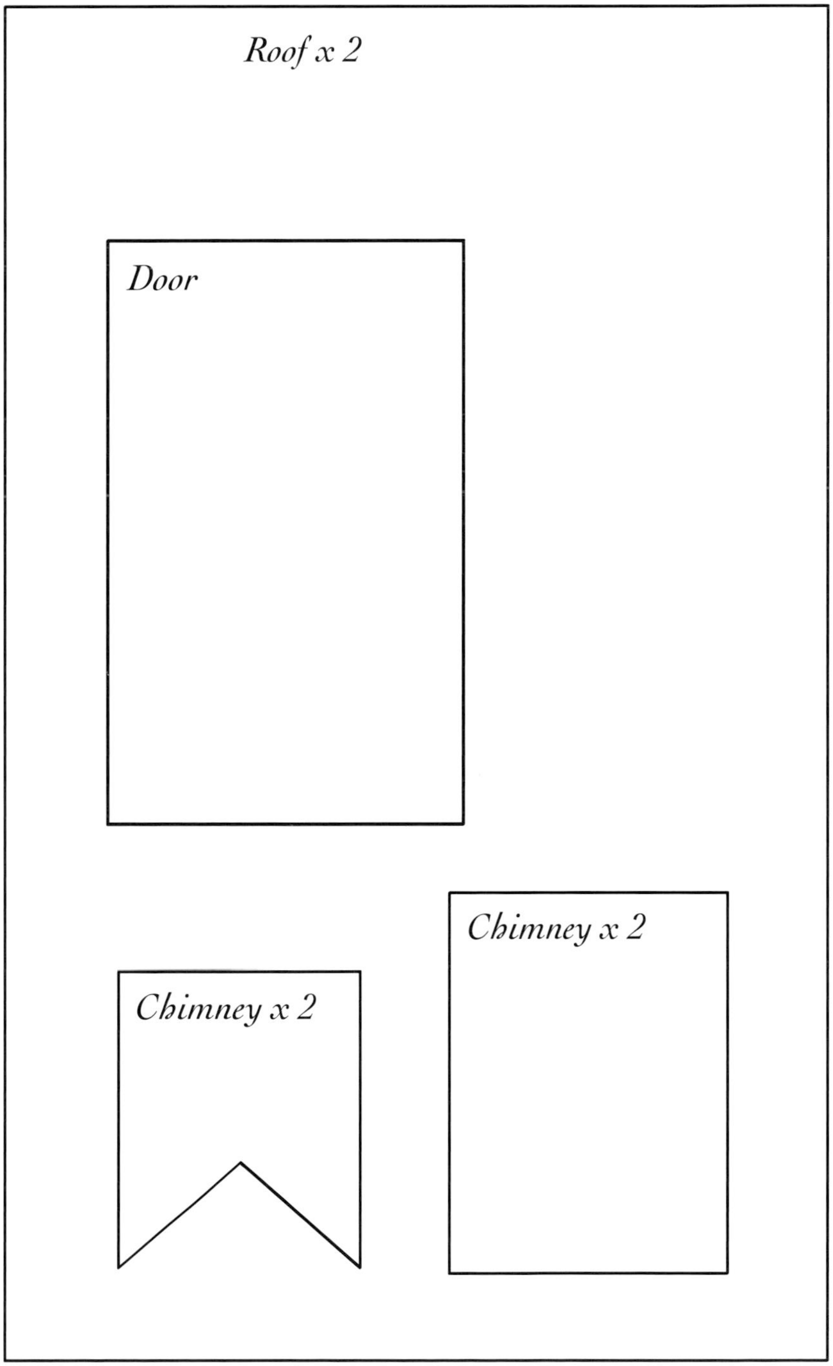

Roof x 2

Door

Chimney x 2

Chimney x 2

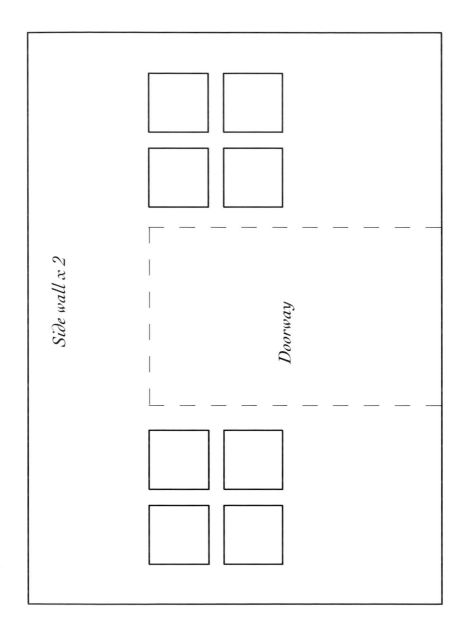

Side wall x 2

Doorway

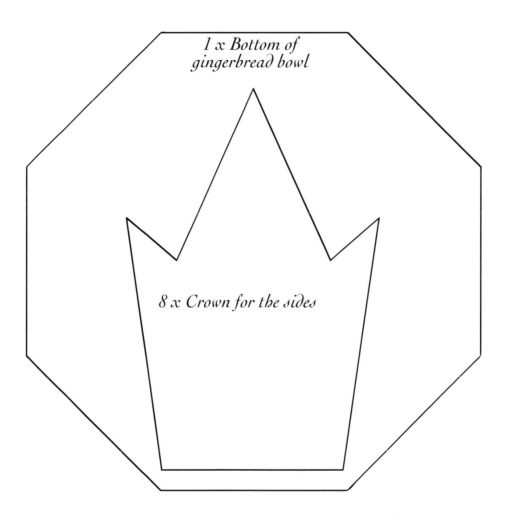

1 x Bottom of gingerbread bowl

8 x Crown for the sides

Recipe Index